AF575365

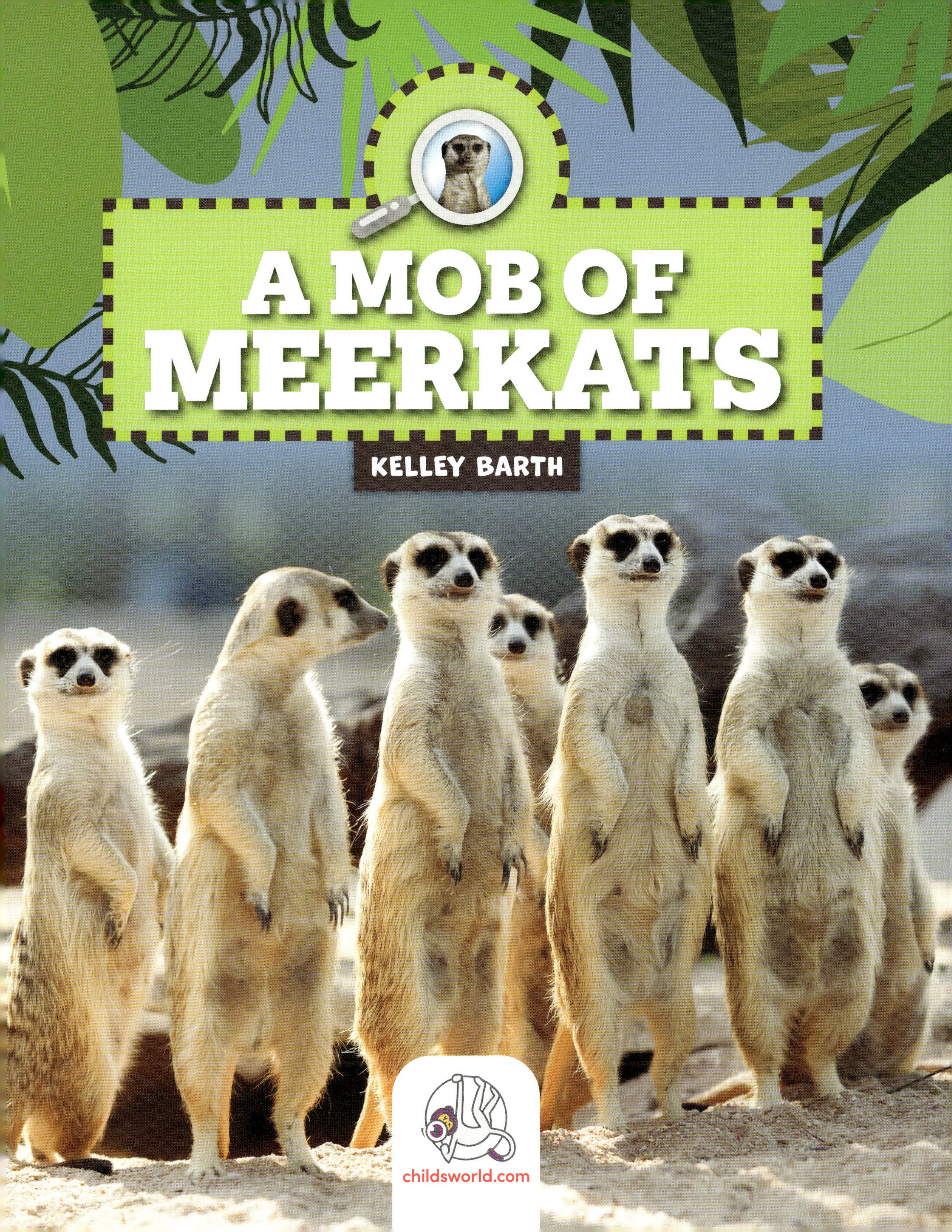
A MOB OF
MEERKATS
KELLEY BARTH
childsworld.com

Published by The Child's World®
800-599-READ • www.childsworld.com

Photography Credits
page 1: ©nattanan726/Getty Images; page 1: ©kevdog818/Getty Images; page 5: ©bucky_za/Getty Images; page 6: ©Winfried Wisniewski/Getty Images;page 10: ©Paul C Stokes/Getty Images; page 12: ©chain45154/Getty Images; page 15: ©mcbrugg/Getty Images; page 16: ©EcoPic /Getty Images; page 22: ©FotoDuets/Getty Images

ISBN Information
9781503884991 (Reinforced Library Binding)
9781503885882 (Portable Document Format)
9781503886520 (Online Multi-user eBook)
9781503887169 (Electronic Publication)

LCCN 2023937349

Printed in the United States of America

Kelley Barth is a former children's librarian who loves connecting with young people over stories and books. When she isn't busy writing, Kelley enjoys reading, hiking, crafting, and exploring national parks. She lives in Minnesota with her husband and dog.

TABLE OF CONTENTS

CHAPTER 1

Meet the Mob

The sun has risen over Africa's Kalahari Desert. A family of meerkats peeks out of their underground **burrow**. One meerkat keeps watch for danger while the others begin searching for insects to eat. Suddenly, the lookout howls a warning. His cry alerts the rest of the group. A hungry eagle is flying above, so the meerkat family dives quickly back underground to the safety of their burrow. A narrow escape, they live to see another day.

Meerkats live in burrows that are like underground houses. They have multiple "rooms," several "doors," and lots of tunnels that connect all the parts of the burrow.

Alpha is the first letter of the Greek alphabet. It has come to mean "first," and an alpha is considered a leader.

A group of meerkats is called a **mob**. They are also sometimes called a gang or a band. A *mob* is a large crowd of people that may cause trouble or violence. This mob behavior is one way meerkats defend themselves from threats. A mob of meerkats will hiss and growl as they rock back and forth together to scare away a snake or an outsider meerkat.

Mobs usually have anywhere between ten and fifty meerkats. Each mob is led by an **alpha** female. The alpha female chooses an alpha male and together they rule the mob. All other adult meerkats in the mob are known as **beta** females or beta males.

Meerkat mobs live in the Kalahari and Namib Deserts in southern Africa. These deserts are very hot and dry. Meerkats live in large burrows under the ground. Some mobs work together to dig their burrows in the desert sand. Some mobs use burrows that were dug by other animals. Each burrow is like an underground maze. Tunnels connect larger dens for meerkats to sleep in. Burrows help meerkat mobs stay cool in daytime and warm at night. Living underground also helps meerkats stay safe. Each burrow system has a number of entrances throughout their **territory**. If a **predator** appears, meerkats can quickly slip inside any small burrow entrance.

AFRICA
Atlantic Ocean
Indian Ocean
KEY
Where meerkats live

CHAPTER 2

All in the Family

Mating in a meerkat mob can be tricky business. The alpha female is the only meerkat allowed to mate and have babies. When she is ready to mate, she will chase all of the other female meerkats away from the mob. About 11 weeks after the alpha female and male mate, the mother meerkat will give birth. Baby meerkats are called pups. Meerkats usually have two to five pups at a time. They can have up to four **litters** of pups each year.

After the alpha female's pups are born, the other adult females may return to the mob. Many will return but some females join other mobs.

At birth, a meerkat pup is about the size of a Matchbox car. They weigh about as much as a slice of bread.

REALITY TV

You've heard of reality shows about families and movie stars... but meerkats? *Meerkat Manor* was a show that followed a large mob of meerkats living in the Kalahari Desert. The show lasted four seasons and aired on Animal Planet in the US. *Meerkat Manor* showed viewers how one meerkat mob interacted with each other and with other mobs, as well as other desert animals. The show allowed scientists a closeup view of meerkat relationships, communication, family drama, and eating and grooming behaviors.

MEERKAT MENTORS

Young meerkats have a lot to learn from their elder **mentors**. Mentors teach pups basic skills to survive, such as how to disarm a scorpion—one of meerkats' favorite foods. Like human adults, mentors start young meerkats off with easy tasks. They teach the youngsters how to remove a stinger from a dead scorpion first—much easier when the scorpion isn't moving! Then, they show them how to remove a stinger from an injured scorpion. The young meerkat learns that the stinger has to be removed before they eat a scorpion. Once they learn to remove the stinger, the young meerkats are allowed to kill scorpions on their own.

Meerkat pups drink their mother's milk for around nine weeks.

After a new litter is born, the entire mob works together to help raise the young pups. Pups are born blind and helpless. When the mother meerkat isn't nursing her pups, older siblings help babysit. Newborn pups are under constant watch inside the safety of the burrow. After a few weeks, pups follow their babysitters into the world and learn how to **forage** for food. Once they are old enough, young meerkats begin to learn important life skills from a mentor meerkat. After two to three years, most meerkats will leave their family to start a new mob of their own.

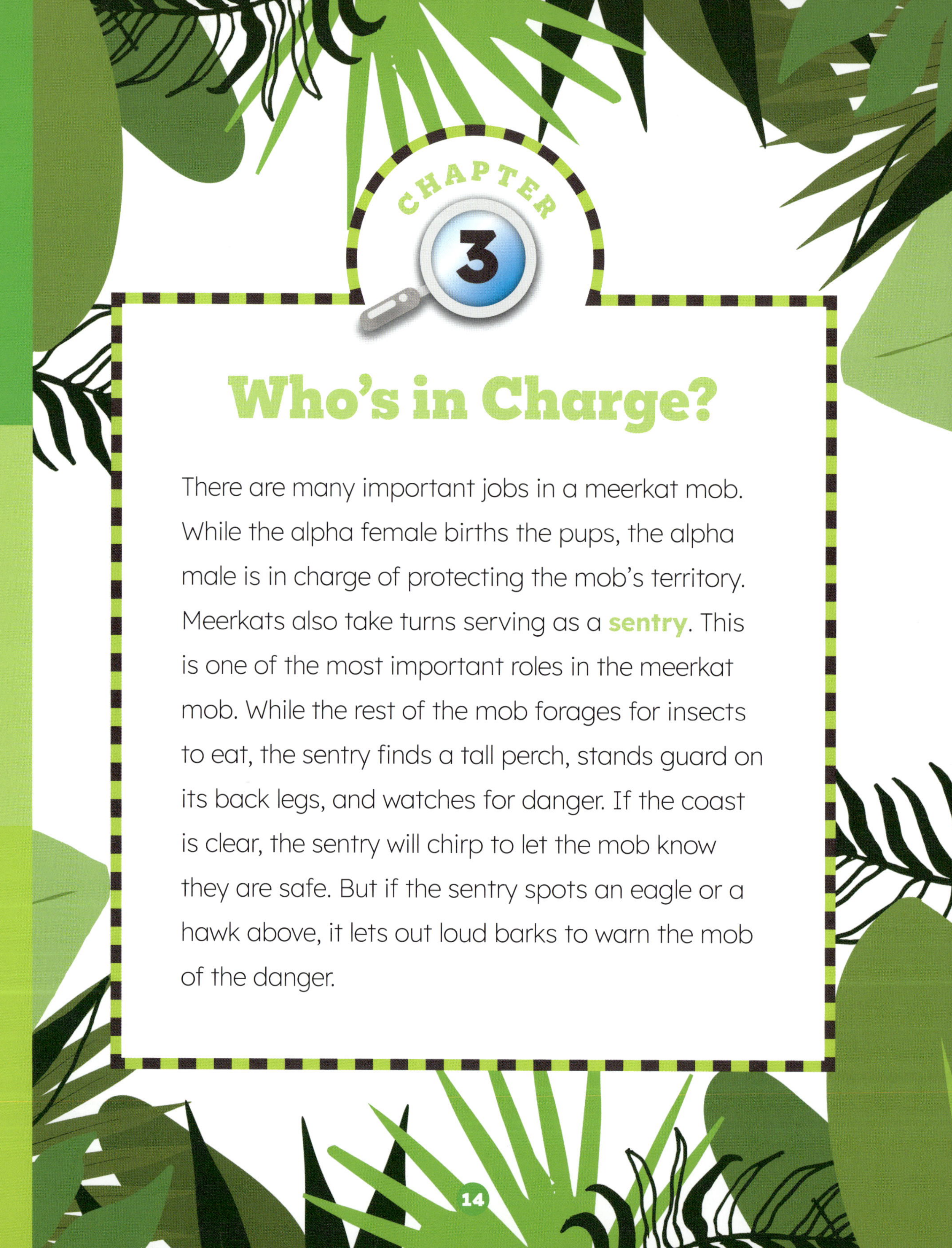

Who's in Charge?

There are many important jobs in a meerkat mob. While the alpha female births the pups, the alpha male is in charge of protecting the mob's territory. Meerkats also take turns serving as a **sentry**. This is one of the most important roles in the meerkat mob. While the rest of the mob forages for insects to eat, the sentry finds a tall perch, stands guard on its back legs, and watches for danger. If the coast is clear, the sentry will chirp to let the mob know they are safe. But if the sentry spots an eagle or a hawk above, it lets out loud barks to warn the mob of the danger.

A meerkat stands watch as sentry for about an hour. Then, another meerkat in the mob takes over.

Meerkats are good at digging holes. They dig for insects to eat and to make new burrows.

There are many tasks to do each day, so meerkat mobs are always busy. When they aren't searching for food, meerkats work together to dig new tunnels and keep their burrows clean. Meerkats also strengthen their bonds by grooming each other. They pick ticks and fleas out of each other's fur to stay clean and healthy. Play-fighting also helps the mob. Young meerkats play to practice their foraging and defense skills. Older meerkats also play-fight to show their **dominance** in the mob.

CHAPTER 4

What Makes Mobs Unique?

Meerkat mobs are unique in the animal world. Every meerkat knows its place in the mob's **hierarchy**. In the mob, there is always a balance of cooperation and aggression. All meerkats must cooperate and work together to find food and stay safe. But the alpha female in the mob is also very aggressive. She makes sure that her pups have the best chance at survival.

She also leads the mob as they travel looking for food. But if the mob comes to a busy human road, the alpha female will force a lower-ranking meerkat to cross the road first. This way the alpha female avoids the danger of speeding cars.

Meerkat Size Comparison

Meerkats are around 11 inches (29 centimeters) long. They weigh less than 2.2 pounds (1 kilogram).

The average gray squirrel is 8–10 inches (20–25 cm) long and weighs around 1.5 pounds (.68 kg).

CHAPTER 5

Why Mobs Matter

Living in a desert environment is hard work. But living together in groups helps meerkats in many ways. There is safety in numbers. Larger mobs are often able to fight for the best territories and have better access to food and water. Large meerkat mobs also have more resources to raise healthy pups and keep a close eye out for danger. Living and working together as a group is part of what makes meerkats so special. Similar to a human neighborhood, a mob of meerkats works and plays together and helps keep their community safe!

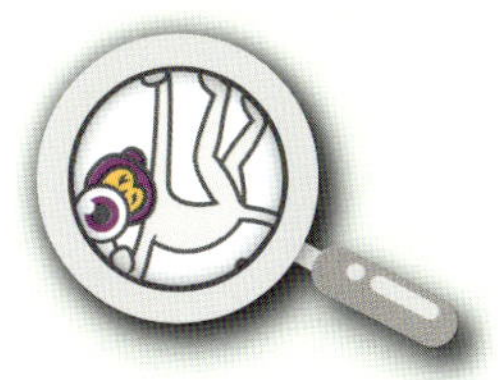

Wonder More

Wondering about New Information

What new information did you learn about meerkat mobs? Write down three new facts that you learned. Did this information surprise you? Why or why not?

Wondering How It Matters

Living in larger groups helps meerkats stay safe. How does living and working in a family help you? Why is it important for meerkats to live and work together as a group?

Wondering Why

Why do you think living in a mob is helpful to meerkats? Why are they important? What are some of the different jobs and roles that exist in a meerkat mob?

Ways to Keep Wondering

After reading this book, what questions do you have about meerkat mobs? What can you do to learn more about them?

Design a Meerkat Burrow

What You Need:

- paper
- pencil or pen
- crayons, colored pencils, markers (optional)

Steps to Take:

1. Design and draw your underground meerkat burrow. Make sure to include underground dens for the meerkats to sleep in and plenty of holes at the surface so your meerkats have safe escape routes.

2. Add your mob into the picture. What is each meerkat doing?

3. Label your meerkats with their role. Don't forget to include all of the different roles in the mob. Where are the alpha female and alpha male? Are there pups with babysitters? Where is the sentry?

Glossary

alpha (AL-fuh) An alpha is someone or something that is first in position or ranking.

beta (BAY-tuh) A beta is someone or something that is second in position or ranking.

burrow (BUR-oh) Burrows are holes in the ground made by animals for shelter.

dominance (DOM-ih-nuntz) Dominance is the power of one animal over another.

forage (FOR-ij) To forage is to search or look for food.

hierarchy (HY-ur-ar-kee) A hierarchy is a group organized into orders or ranks.

litter (LIT-tur) A litter is a group of baby animals born at the same time.

mating (MAYT-ing) Animals that are mating are joining together to produce offspring.

mentor (MEN-tor) A mentor is an older individual that trains and teaches younger members of a family, team, or other group.

mob (MOB) A mob is a large, disorderly crowd of people.

predator (PREH-duh-tuhr) A predator is an animal that hunts other animals for food.

sentry (SEN-tree) A sentry stands guard and alerts the group to danger.

territory (TAYR-ih-tor-ee) Territory is the physical area that an animal or group lives on or defends.

Find Out More

In the Library

Emminizer, Theresa. *Burrowing Meerkats.* New York, NY: PowerKids Press, 2021.

Nelson, Penelope. *Meerkats.* Minneapolis, MN: Bullfrog Books, 2020.

Riggs, Kate. *Meerkats.* Mankato, MN: Creative Education, 2023.

On the Web

Visit our website for links about meerkat mobs:
childsworld.com/links

Note to Parents, Caregivers, Teachers, and Librarians: We routinely verify our web links to make sure they are safe and active sites. So encourage your readers to check them out!

Index